SENECA ON PROVIDENCE, MODER
AND CONSTANCY OF MIND
Part Two of *Seneca of a Happy Life*
by Roger L'Estrange ✸ Edited and Revised by Keith Seddon

Roger L'Estrange, staunch royalist, author and pamphleteer, one-time inmate of Newgate Prison, one-time exile, one-time Member of Parliament, takes up the teaching of the Roman Stoic philosopher Seneca, rearranging and paraphrasing the original Latin to shape a unique and engaging work of his own.

Although it is not in our power to prevent fortune from sending us perils and trials, we may yet meet them with courage, free of perturbation, and bear them as unkind seasons, neither frightened of terrors nor grieving for lost pleasures.

This slim volume is the second of three parts of Roger L'Estrange's *Seneca of a Happy Life*, being itself an extract of a much larger whole, *Seneca's Morals*, first published in 1678.

Keith Seddon is professor of philosophy at Warnborough College Ireland.

Roger L'Estrange's *Seneca of a Happy Life* (an extract from *Seneca's Morals By Way of Abstract: To which is added, A Discourse, under the Title of An After-Thought*), edited and revised by Keith Seddon, in Three Parts:

OTHER BOOKS BY KEITH SEDDON:

Epictetus: The Discourses, Handbook and Fragments [forthcoming]
The Stoic Fragments of Epictetus [forthcoming]
An Outline of Cynic Philosophy: Antisthenes of Athens and Diogenes of Sinope in Diogenes Laertius Book Six (with C. D. Yonge)
A Summary of Stoic Philosophy: Zeno of Citium in Diogenes Laertius Book Seven (with C. D. Yonge)
Stoic Serenity: A Practical Course on Finding Inner Peace
Epictetus' Handbook and the Tablet of Cebes: Guides to Stoic Living
Lao Tzu: Tao Te Ching
Learning the Tao: Chuang Tzu as Teacher
Tractatus Philosophicus Tao: A short treatise on the Tao Te Ching of Lao Tzu
Time: A Philosophical Treatment

SENECA

ON PROVIDENCE, MODERATION,

AND CONSTANCY OF MIND

Part Two

of

Seneca of a Happy Life

An Extract from

SENECA'S MORALS

by

Roger L'Estrange

Edited and Revised by Keith Seddon

LULU

Seneca of a Happy Life, part of *Seneca's Morals By way of Abstract:
To which is added, A Discourse, under the Title of An After-Thought*
by Roger L'Estrange, was first published in 1678.

This new edition first published 2010
by Keith Seddon
at Lulu
www.lulu.com

Typeset in Bembo Book 12/15 pt

ISBN 978–0–955–6844–9–4 (paperback)

It is only philosophy that makes the mind invincible and places us out of the reach of fortune, so that all her arrows fall short of us.

CONTENTS

CHAPTER 8

THE DUE CONTEMPLATION OF
DIVINE PROVIDENCE IS THE
CERTAIN CURE OF ALL
MISFORTUNES

WHOEVER observes the world and the order of it will find all the motions in it to be only a vicissitude of falling and rising; nothing extinguished, and even those things which seem to us to perish are in truth but changed. The seasons go and return, day and night follow in their courses, the heavens roll, and Nature goes on with her work: all things succeed in their turns, storms, and calms; the law of Nature will have it so, which we must follow and obey, accounting all things that are done to be well done, so that what we cannot mend we must suffer, and wait upon Providence without repining. It is the part of a cowardly soldier to follow his commander groaning, but a generous man delivers himself up to God without struggling, and it is only for a narrow mind to condemn the order of the world, and to propound rather the mending of Nature than of himself. No man has any cause of complaint against Providence, if that which is right pleases him. Those glories that appear fair to the eye, their lustre is but false and superficial, and they are only vanity and delusion: they are rather the goods of a dream than a substantial possession; they may cozen us at a distance, but bring them once to the touch, they are rotten and

9

counterfeit. There are no greater wretches in the world than many of those which the people take to be happy. Those are the only true and incorruptible comforts that will abide all trials; and the more we turn and examine them, the more valuable we find them – and the greatest felicity of all is not to stand in need of any. What is *poverty*? No man lives so poor as he was born. What is *pain*? It will either have an end itself, or make an end of us. In short, fortune has no weapon that reaches the mind: but the bounties of Providence are certain and permanent blessings, and they are the greater and the better, the longer we consider them: that is to say, *The power of contemning things terrible, and despising what the common people covet.* In the very methods of Nature we cannot but observe the regard that Providence had to the good of mankind, even in the disposition of the world, in providing so amply for our maintenance and satisfaction. It is not possible for us to comprehend what the Power is which has made all things: some few sparks of that Divinity are discovered, but infinitely the greater part of it lies hid. We are all of us however thus far agreed; first, in the acknowledgment and belief of that almighty Being and, secondly, that we are to ascribe to it all majesty and goodness.

IF there be a Providence, say some, *how comes it to pass that good men labour under affliction and adversity, and wicked men enjoy themselves in ease and plenty?* My answer is that God deals by us as a good father does by his children; he tries us, he hardens us, and

How comes it that good men are afflicted in this world, and wicked men prosper

fits us for himself. He keeps a strict hand over those that he loves, and by the rest he does as we do by our selves; he lets them go on in license and boldness. As the master gives his most hopeful scholars the hardest lessons, so does God deal with the most generous spirits; and the cross encounters of fortune, we are not to look upon as a cruelty, but as a contest. The familiarity of dangers brings us to the contempt of them, and that part is strongest which is most exercised: the seaman's hand is callous, the soldier's arm is strong, and the tree that is most exposed to the wind takes the best root. There are people that live in a perpetual winter, in extremity of frost and penury, where a cave, a lock of straw, or a few leaves, is all their covering, and wild beasts their nourishment. All this by custom is not only made tolerable, but when it is once taken up upon necessity, by little and little it becomes pleasant to them. Why should we then count that condition of life a calamity which is the lot of many nations? There is no state of life so miserable but there are in it remissions, diversions, nay, and delights too, such is the benignity of Nature toward us, even in the severest accidents of human life. There were no living if adversity should hold on as it begins, and keep up the force of the first impression. We are apt to murmur at many things as great evils that have nothing at all of evil in them besides the complaint, which we should more reasonably take up against ourselves. If I be sick, it is part of my fate; and for other calamities they are usual things; they ought to be; nay, which is more, they must be, for they come by divine appointment. So that we should not only submit to God, but assent to him, and obey him out of *duty*, even if there were no *necessity*. All those terrible appearances that make us groan and tremble are but the tribute of life; we are neither to wish, nor to ask, nor to hope to escape them; for it is a kind of dishonesty to pay a tribute unwillingly. Am I troubled with the stone, or afflicted with continual losses? Nay, is my body in danger? All this is no more than what I prayed for when I prayed for old age. All these things are as familiar in a long life as dust and dirt in a long way. Life is a warfare, and what brave man would not rather choose to be in a tent than in a shambles? Fortune does like a swordsman, she scorns to encounter a fearful man: there is no honour in the victory where there is no danger in the way to it. She tries *Mucius* by *fire*, *Rutilius* by *exile*, *Socrates* by *poison*, *Cato* by *death*. It is only in adverse fortune, and in bad times, that we find great examples. *Mucius* thought himself happier with his hand in the flame than if it had been in the bosom of his mistress. *Fabricius* took more pleasure in eating the roots of his own planting than in all the delicacies of luxury and expense. Shall we call *Rutilius* miserable whom his very enemies have adored? – who, upon a glorious and a public principle, chose rather to lose his country than to return from banishment? – the only man that denied anything to *Sylla* the dictator who recalled him. Nor did he only refuse to come, but drew himself further off: *Let them*, says he, *that think banishment a misfortune, live slaves at Rome, under the imperial cruelties of* Sylla: *he that sets a price upon the heads of senators, and after a law of his own institution against cut-throats, becomes the greatest himself.* Is it not better for a man to live in exile abroad, than to be massacred at home? In suffering for virtue, it is not the torment but the cause that we are to consider; and the more pain, the more renown. When any hardship befalls us, we must look upon it as an act of Providence, which many times suffers particulars to be wounded for the conservation of the whole: beside that, God chastises some people under an appearance of blessing them, turning their prosperity to their ruin, as a punishment for abusing his goodness. And we are farther to consider that many a good man is afflicted, only to teach others to suffer; for we are born for example. And likewise, that where men are contumacious and refractory, it pleases God many times to cure greater evils by less, and to turn our miseries to our advantage.

HOW many casualties and difficulties are there that we dread as insupportable mischiefs, *Prudence* which upon further thoughts, we find to *draws good* be mercies and benefits? As banishment, *out of evil* poverty, loss of relations, sickness, disgrace? Some are cured by the lance, by fire, hunger, thirst; taking out of bones, lopping off limbs, and the like. Nor do we only fear things that are many times beneficial to us, but on the other side, we hanker after and pursue things that are deadly and pernicious. We are poisoned in the very pleasures of our luxury, and betrayed to a thousand diseases by the indulging of our palate. To lose a child, or a limb, is only to part with what we have received, and Nature may do what she pleases

13

with her own. We are frail ourselves, and we have received things transitory: that which was given us may be taken away; calamity tries virtue as the fire does gold. Nay, he that lives most at ease is only delayed, not dismissed, and his portion is to come. When we are visited with sickness, or other afflictions, we are not to murmur as if we were ill used; it is a mark of the general's esteem, when he puts us upon a post of danger: we do not say, *My captain uses me ill*; but, *He does me honour*. And so should we say, that are commanded to encounter difficulties, for this is our case with God Almighty.

WHAT, was *Regulus* the worse, because fortune made choice of him for an eminent instance both of faith and patience? He was *Calamity is the trial of virtue* thrown into a case of wood stuck with pointed nails, so that which way soever he turned his body, it rested upon his wounds; his eyelids were cut off to keep him waking; and yet *Macænas* was not happier upon his *bed*, than *Regulus* upon his *torments*. Nay, the world is not yet grown so wicked as not to prefer *Regulus* before *Macænas*: and can any man take that to be an evil of which Providence accounted this brave man worthy? *It has pleased God* (says he) *to single me out for an experiment of the force of human nature*. No man knows his own strength or value, but by being put to the proof. The pilot is tried in a storm, the soldier in a battle, the rich man knows not how to behave himself in poverty: he that has lived in popularity and applause knows not how he would bear infamy and reproach; nor he that never has children how he would bear the loss of them. Calamity is the occasion of virtue, and a spur to a great mind. The very apprehension of a wound startles a man when he first bears arms, but an old soldier bleeds boldly, because he knows that a man may lose blood and yet win the day. Nay, many times a calamity turns to our advantage, and great ruins have but made way to greater glories. The crying out of *fire* has many times quieted a fray, and the interposing of a wild beast has parted the thief and the traveller; for we are not at leisure for less mischiefs while we are under the apprehensions of greater. One man's life is saved by a disease; another is arrested and taken out of the way, just when his house was falling upon his head.

TO show now that the favours or the crosses of fortune, and the accidents of sickness and of health, are neither good nor evil, God permits them indifferently both to good *Accidents are neither good nor evil* and evil men. *It is hard*, you will say, *for a virtuous man to suffer all sorts of misery, and for a wicked man not only to go free, but to enjoy himself at pleasure.* And, is it not the same thing for men of prostituted impudence and wickedness to sleep in a whole skin, when men of honour and honesty bear arms, lie in the trenches, and receive wounds? Or for the vestal virgins to rise in the night to their prayers, when common strumpets lie stretching themselves in their beds? We should rather say with *Demetrius, If I had known the will of heaven before I was called to it, I would have offered myself.* If it be the pleasure of God to take my children, I have brought them up to that end: if my fortune, any part of my body, or my life, I would rather present it than yield it up. I am ready to part with all, and to suffer all; for I know that nothing comes to pass but what God appoints: our fate is decreed, and things do not so much happen, as in their due time proceed, and every man's portion of joy and sorrow is predetermined.

THERE is nothing falls amiss to a good man that *Nothing that* can be charged upon Providence; for *is properly* wicked actions, lewd thoughts, ambitious *evil can befall* projects, blind lusts, and insatiable avarice, *a good man* against all these he is armed by the benefit of reason. And, do we expect now that God should look to our luggage too? (I mean our bodies.) *Democritus* discharged himself of his treasure, as the clog and burden of his mind. Shall we wonder then, if God suffers that to befall a good man, which a good man sometimes does to himself? I lose a son, and why not, when it may sometime so fall out that I myself may kill him? Suppose he be banished by an order of state, is it not the same thing with a man's voluntarily leaving of his country, and never to return? Many afflictions may befall a good man, but no evil; for contraries will never incorporate: all the rivers in the world are never able to change the taste or quality of the sea. Prudence and religion are above accidents, and draw good out of everything; affliction keeps a man in use, and makes him strong, patient, and hardy. Providence treats us like a generous father, and brings us up to labours, toils, and dangers; whereas the indulgence of a fond mother makes us weak and spiritless. God loves us with a masculine love, and turns us loose to injuries and indignities: he takes delight to see a brave and a good man wrestling with evil fortune, and yet keeping himself upon his legs, when the whole world is in disorder about him. And are not we ourselves delighted to see a bold fellow press with his lance upon a boar or lion? And the constancy and resolution of the action is the grace and dignity of the spectacle. No man can be happy that does not stand firm against all contingencies; and say to himself in all extremities, *I should have been content, if it might have been so, or so, but since it is otherwise determined, God will provide better.* The more we struggle with our necessities, we draw the knot the harder, and the worse it is with us: and the more the bird flaps and flutters in the snare, the surer she is caught. So that the best way is to submit and lie still, under this double consideration, *that the proceedings of God are unquestionable, and his decrees are not to be resisted.*

CHAPTER 9

OF LEVITY OF MIND, AND OTHER IMPEDIMENTS OF A HAPPY LIFE

NOW to sum up what is already delivered, we have showed what happiness is, and wherein it consists,* that it is founded upon wisdom and virtue,† for we must first know what we ought to do, and then live according to that knowledge. We have also discoursed the helps of philosophy and precepts towards a *happy life*,‡ the blessing of a good conscience;§ that a good man can never be miserable, nor a wicked man happy,** nor any man unfortunate that cheerfully submits to Providence.†† We shall now examine how it comes to pass, that when the certain way to happiness lies so fair before us, men will yet steer their course on the other side, which as manifestly leads to ruin.

THERE are some that live without any design at all, and only pass in the world like straws *Impediments to happiness* upon a river; they do not go, but they are carried. Others only deliberate upon the parts of life, and not upon the whole, which is a great error, for there is no disposing of the circumstances of it, unless we first propound the main scope. How shall

---

* In Chapter 1.
† In Chapters 2 and 3.
‡ In Chapters 4 and 5.
§ In Chapter 6.
** In Chapter 7.
†† In Chapter 8, above.

any man take his aim without a mark? Or, what wind will serve him that is not yet resolved upon his port? We live as it were by chance, and by chance we are governed. Some there are that torment themselves afresh with the memory of what is past: *Lord! What did I endure? Never was any man in my condition, everybody gave me over, my very heart was ready to break, &c.* Others again afflict themselves with the apprehension of evils to come, and very ridiculously both: for the *one* does not *now* concern us, and the *other, not yet.* Beside that, there may be remedies for mischiefs likely to happen, for they give us warning by signs and symptoms of their approach. Let him that would be quiet, take heed not to provoke men that are in power, but live without giving offence; and if we cannot make all great men our friends, it will suffice to keep them from being our enemies. This is a thing we must avoid, as a mariner would do a storm. A rash seaman never considers what wind blows, or what course he steers, but runs at a venture, as if he would brave the rocks and the eddies; whereas he that is careful and considerate, informs himself beforehand where the danger lies and what weather it is like to be: he consults his compass, and keeps aloof from those places that are infamous for wrecks and miscarriages. So does a wise man in the common business of life; he keeps out of the way from those that may do him hurt, but it is a point of prudence not to let them take notice that he does it on purpose; for that which a man shuns, he tacitly condemns. Let him have a care also of *listeners, newsmongers* and *medlers* in other people's matters; for their discourse is commonly of such things as are never profitable, and most commonly dangerous, either to be spoken or heard.

LEVITY of mind is a great hindrance of repose, *Levity of mind is* and the very changeability of wicked-*a great hindrance* ness is an addition to the wickedness *of our repose* itself, for it is inconstancy added to iniquity: we relinquish the thing we sought, and then we take it up again, and so divide our lives between our lust and our repentances. From one appetite we pass to another, not so much upon choice, as for change; and there is a check of conscience that casts a damp upon all our unlawful pleasures, which makes us lose the day in expectation of that night, and the night itself for fear of the approaching light. Some people are *never* quiet, others are *always* so, and they are both to blame: for that which looks like vivacity and industry in one, is only a restlessness and agitation; and that which passes in the other for moderation and reserve, is but a drowsy and an unactive sloth. Let motion and rest both take their turns according to the order of Nature, which make both the day and the night. Some are perpetually shifting from one thing to another. Others again make their whole life but a kind of uneasy sleep. Some lie tossing and turning, until very weariness brings them to rest. Others again I cannot so properly call inconstant, as lazy. There are many proprieties and diversities of vice, but it is one never-failing effect of it, to live displeased. We do all of us labour under inordinate desires; we are either timorous and dare not venture, or venturing we do not succeed, or else we cast ourselves upon uncertain hopes where we are perpetually solicitous and in suspense. In this distraction, we are apt to propose to ourselves things dishonest and hard, and when we have taken great pains to no purpose, we come then to repent of our undertakings. We are afraid to go on, and we can neither master our appetites nor obey them. We live and die restless and irresolute and, which is worst of all, when we grow weary of the public, and betake ourselves to solitude for relief, our minds are sick and wallowing, and the very house and walls are troublesome to us; we grow impatient, and ashamed of ourselves, and suppress our inward vexation until it breaks our heart for want of vent. This is it that makes us sour and morose, envious of others, and dissatisfied with ourselves, until at last, betwixt our troubles for other people's successes and the despair of our own, we fall foul upon fortune and the times, and get into a corner perhaps, where we sit brooding over our own disquiets. In these dispositions there is a kind of pruriginous fancy that makes some people take delight in labour and uneasiness, like the clawing of an itch until the blood starts.

THIS is it that puts us upon rambling voyages, one while by land, but still disgusted *Change of place* with the present. The town pleases us *does no good* today, the country tomorrow; the splen- *without change* dour of the court at one time, the horrors *of mind* of a wilderness at another; but all this while we carry our plague about us, for it is not the place we are weary of, but ourselves. Nay, our weakness extends to everything, for we are impatient equally of toil and of pleasure. This trotting of the ring, and only treading the same steps over and over again, has made many a man lay violent hands upon himself. It must be the change of the mind, not of the climate, that will remove the heaviness of the heart; our vices go along with us, and we carry in ourselves the causes of our disquiets. There is a great weight lies upon us, and the bare shocking of it makes it the more uneasy; changing of countries, in this case, is not travelling, but wandering. We must keep on our course, if we would gain our journey's end. *He that cannot live happily anywhere, will live happily nowhere.* What is a man the better for travelling, as if his cares could not find him out wherever he goes? Is there any retiring from the fear of death, or of torments, or from those difficulties which beset a man wherever he is? It is only philosophy that makes the mind invincible and places us out of the reach of fortune, so that all her arrows fall short of us. This it is that reclaims the rage of our lusts, and sweetens the anxiety of our fears. Frequent changing of places, or counsels, shows an instability of mind; and we must fix the body before we can fix the soul. We can hardly stir abroad, or look about us, without encountering something or other that revives our appetites. As he that would cast off an unhappy love avoids whatsoever may put him in mind of the person, so he that would wholly deliver himself from his beloved lusts must shun all objects that may put them in his head again, and remind him of them. We travel, as children run up and down after strange sights, for

22

novelty, not profit; we return neither the be
the sounder; nay, and the very agitation hurts u.
learn to call towns and places by their names, and
tell stories of mountains, and of rivers but, had not our
time been better spent in the study of wisdom, and of
virtue, in the learning of what is already discovered,
and in the quest of things not yet found out? If a man
break his leg, or strain his ankle, he sends presently for
a surgeon to set all right again, and does not take horse
upon it, or put himself on shipboard: no more does the
change of place work upon our disordered minds than
upon our bodies. It is not the place, I hope, that makes
either an orator, or a physician. Will any man ask
upon the road, Pray which is the way to prudence, to
justice, to temperance, to fortitude? No matter whith-
er any man goes that carries his affections along with
him. He that would make his travels delightful, must
make himself a temperate companion. A great traveller
was complaining that he was never the better for his
travels. *That is very true,* said *Socrates, because you
travelled with yourself.* Now, had not he better have
made himself another man, than to transport himself
to another place? It is no matter what manners we find
anywhere, so long as we carry our own. But we have
all of us a natural curiosity of seeing fine sights, and of
making new discoveries, turning over antiquities,
learning the customs of nations, *&c.* We are never
quiet: today we seek an office, tomorrow we are sick
of it. We divide our lives betwixt a dislike of the present and a desire of the future; but he that lives as he
should orders himself so as neither to fear nor to wish

for tomorrow; if it come, it is welcome, but if not, there is nothing lost, for that which is come is but the same over again with what is past. As levity is a pernicious enemy to quiet, so pertinacy is a great one too. The one changes nothing, the other sticks to nothing; and which of the two is the worse may be a question. It is many times seen that we beg earnestly for those things which, if they were offered us, we would refuse: and it is but just to punish this easiness of asking with an equal facility of granting. There are some things we would be thought to desire, which we are so far from desiring, that we dread them. *I shall tire you,* says one in the middle of a tedious story. *No, pray be pleased to go on,* we cry, though we wished his tongue out at half way. Nay, we do not deal candidly even with God himself. We should say to ourselves, in these cases, *This I have drawn upon myself. I could never be quiet, until I had gotten this woman, this place, this estate, this honour; and now see what is become of it.*

ONE sovereign remedy against all misfortunes is constancy of mind. The changing of parties and countenances looks as if a man were driven with the wind. Nothing can be above him that is above fortune. It is not violence, reproach, contempt, or whatever else from without, that can make a wise man quit his ground, but he is proof against calamities, both great and small. Only our error is that what we cannot do ourselves, we think nobody else can, so that we judge of the wise by the measures of the weak. Place me among princes, or among beggars; the one shall not make me proud, nor

Constancy of mind secures us in all difficulties

the other ashamed. I can take as sound a sleep in a barn as in a palace, and a bottle of hay makes me as good a lodging as a bed of down. Should every day succeed to my wish, it should not transport me; nor would I think myself miserable, if I should not have one quiet hour in my whole life. I will not transport myself with either pain or pleasure; but yet for all that, I could wish that I had an easier game to play, and that I were put rather to moderate my joys than my sorrows. If I were am imperial prince, I had rather take, than be taken: and yet I would bear the same mind under the chariot of my conqueror, that I had in my own. It is no great matter to trample upon those things that are most coveted or feared by the common people. There are those that will laugh upon the wheel, and cast themselves upon a certain death, only upon a transport of love, perhaps anger, avarice, or revenge – how much more then upon an instinct of virtue, which is invincible and steady? If a short obstinacy of mind can do this, how much more shall a composed and a deliberate virtue, whose force is equal and perpetual?

TO secure ourselves in this world, first, we must aim at nothing that men count worth *The less we have* the wrangling for; secondly, we must *to do with the* not value the possession of anything *world, the better* which even a common thief would think worth the stealing. A man's body is no booty. Let the way be never so dangerous for robberies, the poor and the naked pass quietly. A plain-dealing sincerity of manners makes a man's life happy, even in despite of scorn and contempt, which is every clear man's fate. But we had better yet be contemned for simplicity than lie perpetually upon the torture of a counterfeit, provided that care be taken not to confound simplicity with negligence. And it is moreover an uneasy life, that of a disguise, for a man to seem to be what he is not, to keep a perpetual guard upon himself, and to live in fear of discovery. He takes every man that looks upon him for a spy, over and above the trouble of being put to play another man's part. It is a good remedy in some cases for a man to apply himself to civil affairs and public business; and yet, in this state of life too, what betwixt ambition and calumny, it is hardly safe to be honest. There are indeed some cases wherein a wise man will give way; but let him not yield over-easily neither: if he marches off, let him have a care of his honour, and make his retreat with his sword in his hand, and his face to the enemy. Of all others, a studious life is the least tiresome; it makes us easy to ourselves and to others, and gains us both friends and reputation.

CHAPTER 10

HE THAT SETS UP HIS REST UPON CONTINGENCIES SHALL NEVER BE QUIET

NEVER pronounce any man happy that depends upon fortune for his happiness, for nothing can be more preposterous than to place the good of a reasonable creature in unreasonable things. If I have lost anything it was adventitious; and the less money, the less trouble; the less favour, the less envy: nay, even in those cases that put us out of our wits, it is not the loss itself, but the opinion of the loss that troubles us. It is a common mistake to account those things necessary that are superfluous, and to depend upon fortune for the felicity of life, which arises only from virtue. There is no trusting to her smiles; the sea swells and rages in a moment, and the ships are swallowed up at night, in the very place where they sported themselves in the morning. And fortune has the same power over princes that it has over empires; over nations that it has over cities; and the same power over cities that it has over private men. Where is that estate that may not be followed upon the heel with famine and beggary? That dignity which the next moment may not be laid in the dust? That kingdom that is secure from desolation and ruin? The period of all things is at hand, as well that which casts out the fortunate as the other that delivers the unhappy; and that which may fall out at any time may

27

fall out this very day. What *shall* come to pass I know not, but what *may* come to pass I know: so that I will despair of nothing, but expect everything; and whatsoever Providence remits is clear gain. Every moment, if it spares me, deceives me; and yet in some sort it does not deceive me, for though I know that anything may happen, yet I know likewise that everything will not. I will hope the best, and provide for the worst. Methinks we should not find so much fault with fortune for her inconstancy when we ourselves suffer a change every moment that we live; only other changes make more noise, and this steals upon us like the shadow upon a dial, every jot as certainly, but more insensibly.

THE burning of *Lyons* may serve to show us that we are never safe, and to arm us against all surprises. The terror of it must needs be great, for the calamity is almost without example. If it had been fired by an enemy, the flame would have left some further mischief to have been done by the soldiers. But to be wholly consumed, we have not heard of many earthquakes so pernicious, so many rarities to be destroyed in one night, and in the depth of peace to suffer an outrage beyond the extremity of war – who would believe it? But twelve hours betwixt so fair a city and none at all: it was laid in ashes in less time than it would require to tell the story. To stand unshaken in such a calamity is hardly to be expected, and our wonder cannot but be equal to our grief. Let this accident teach us to provide against all possibilities that

An influence of the uncertainty of human affairs in the burning of Lyons

28

fall within the power of fortune. All external things are under her dominion: one while she calls our hands to her assistance, another while she contents herself with her own force, and destroys us with mischiefs of which we cannot find the author. No time, place, or condition is excepted. She makes our very pleasures painful to us. She makes war upon us in the depth of peace, and turns the means of our security into an occasion of fear. She turns a friend into an enemy, and makes a foe of a companion. We suffer the effects of war without any adversary, and rather than fail, our felicity shall be the cause of our destruction. Lest we should either forget or neglect her power, every day produces something extraordinary. She persecutes the most temperate with sickness, the strongest constitutions with the phthisic; she brings the innocent to punishment, and the most retired she assaults with tumults. Those glories that have grown up with many ages, with infinite labour and expense, and under the favour of many auspicious providences, one day scatters, and brings to nothing. He that pronounced a day, nay, an hour, sufficient for the destruction of the greatest empire, might have fallen to a moment. It were some comfort yet to the frailty of mankind and of human affairs, if things might but decay as slowly as they rise; but they grow by degrees, and they fall to ruin in an instant. There is no felicity in anything either private or public; men, nations, and cities, have all their fates and periods. Our very entertainments are not without terror, and our calamity rises there where we least expect it. Those kingdoms that stood the

shock both of foreign wars and civil, come to destruction without the sight of an enemy. Nay, we are to
dread our peace and felicity more than violence, because we are there taken unprovided; unless in a state
of peace we do the duty of men in war, and say to
ourselves, *Whatsoever may be, will be.* I am today safe
and happy in the love of my country; I am tomorrow
banished. Today in pleasure, peace, health; tomorrow
broken upon the wheel, led in triumph, and in the ag-
ony of sickness. Let us therefore prepare for a ship-
wreck in the port, and for a tempest in a calm. One
violence drives me from my country, another ravishes
that from me; and that very place where a man can
hardly pass this day for a crowd, may be tomorrow a
desert. Wherefore let us set before our eyes the whole
condition of human nature, and consider as well what
may happen, as what commonly *does.* The way to make
future calamities easy to us in the sufferance, is to
make them familiar to us in the contemplation. How
many cities in *Asia, Achaia, Assyria, Macedonia,* have
been swallowed up by earthquakes? Nay, whole countries are lost, and large provinces laid under water; but
time brings all things to an end, for all the works of
mortals are mortal; all possessions and their possessors
are uncertain and perishable; and what wonder is it to
lose anything at any time, when we must one day lose
all?

THAT which we call our own is but lent us, and
That which we what we have received *gratis* we must
call our own is return without complaint. That which
but lent us fortune gives us this hour, she may take

30

away the next; and he that trusts to her favours shall either find himself deceived, or if he be not, he will at least be troubled because he may be so. There is no defence in walls, fortifications, and engines, against the power of fortune. We must provide ourselves within, and when we are safe there, we are invincible; we may be battered, but not taken. She throws her gifts among us, and we sweat and scuffle for them, never considering how few are the better for that which is expected by all. Some are transported with what they get; others tormented for what they miss; and many times there is a leg or an arm broken in a contest for a counter. She gives us honours, riches, favours, only to take them away again, either by violence or treachery, so that they frequently turn to the damage of the receiver. She throws out baits for us, and sets traps, as we do for birds and beasts; her bounties are snares and lime-twigs to us; we think that we take, but we are taken. If they had anything in them that was substantial, they would some time or other fill and quiet us; but they serve only to provoke our appetite without anything more than pomp and show to allay it. But the best of it is, if a man cannot mend his fortune, he may yet mend his manners, and put himself so far out of her reach, that whether she gives or takes, it shall be all one to us; for we are neither the greater for the one, nor the less for the other. We call this a dark room, or that a light one, when it is in itself neither the one nor the other, but only as the day and the night render it. And so it is in riches, strength of body, beauty, honour, command: and likewise in pain, sickness, banishment, death; which are in themselves middle and indifferent things, and only good or bad as they are influenced by virtue. To weep, lament, and groan, is to renounce our duty; and it is the same weakness on the other side to exult and rejoice. I would rather make my fortune than expect it, being neither depressed with her injuries, nor dazzled with her favours. When *Zeno* was told that all his goods were drowned, *Why then*, says he, *fortune has a mind to make me a philosopher.* It is a great matter for a man to advance his mind above her threats or flatteries; for he that has once gotten the better of her is safe forever.

IT is some comfort yet to the unfortunate, that *Fortune spares* great men lie under the lash for company, *neither great* and that death spares the palace no more *nor small* than the cottage, and that whoever is above me has a power also above him. Do we not daily see funerals without trouble, princes deposed, countries depopulated, towns sacked, without so much as thinking how soon it may be our own case? Whereas, if we would but prepare and arm ourselves against the iniquities of fortune, we should never be surprised. When we see any man banished, beggared, tortured, we are to account, that though the mischief fell upon another, it was levelled at us. What wonder is it if, of so many thousands of dangers that are constantly hovering about us, one comes to hit us at last? That which befalls any man, may befall every man; and then it breaks the force of a present calamity to provide against the future. Whatsoever our lot is, we must bear it; as suppose it be contumely, cruelty, fire, sword,

32

pains, diseases, or a prey to wild beasts; there is no struggling, nor any remedy but moderation. It is to no purpose to bewail any part of our life, when life itself is miserable throughout, and the whole flux of it only a course of transition from one misfortune to another. A man may as well wonder that he should be cold in winter, sick at sea, or have his bones clattered together in a wagon, as at the encounter of ill accidents and crosses in the passage of human life. And it is in vain to run away from fortune, as if there were any hiding-place wherein she could not find us; or to expect any quiet from her, for she makes life a perpetual state of war, without so much as any respite or truce. This we may conclude upon, that her empire is but imaginary, and that whosoever serves her makes himself a voluntary slave, for *the things that are often contemned by the inconsiderate, and always by the wise, are in themselves neither good nor evil*: as pleasure and pains, prosperity and adversity; which can only operate upon our outward condition, without any proper and necessary effect upon the mind.

CHAPTER II

A SENSUAL LIFE IS A MISERABLE LIFE

THE sensuality that we here treat of falls naturally under the head of luxury, which extends to all the excesses of gluttony, lust, effeminacy of manners, and, in short, to whatsoever concerns the over-great care of the carcass.

The excesses of luxury are painful and dangerous

TO begin now with the pleasures of the palate (which deal with us like *Egyptian* thieves, that strangle those they embrace), what shall we say of the luxury of *Nomentanus* and *Apicius*, that entertained their very souls in the kitchen? They have the choicest music for their ears, the most diverting spectacles for their eyes, the choicest variety of meats and drinks for their palates. What is all this, I say, but *a merry madness?* It is true, they have their delights, but not without heavy and anxious thoughts, even in their very enjoyments; besides that they are followed with repentance, and their frolics are little more than the laughter of so many people out of their wits. Their felicities are full of disquiet, and neither sincere nor well grounded. But they have need of one pleasure to support another, and of new prayers to forgive the errors of their former. Their life must needs be wretched, that get with great pains what they keep with greater. One diversion overtakes another. Hope excites hope, ambition begets ambition, so that they only change the matter of their miseries, without seeking any end of them, and shall never be without either prosperous or unhappy causes of disquiet. What if a body might have all the pleasures in the world for the asking? Who would so much un-man himself, as by accepting of them, to desert his soul and become a perpetual slave to his senses? Those false and miserable palates, that judge of meats by the price and difficulty, not by the healthfulness of taste. They vomit that they may eat, and they eat that they may fetch it up again. They cross the seas for rarities, and when they have swallowed them, they will not so much as give them time to digest. Wheresoever Nature has placed men, she has provided them ali-ment. But we rather choose to irritate hunger by ex-pense, than to allay it at an easier rate. What is it that we plough the seas for, or arm ourselves against men and beasts? To what end do we toil and labour, and pile bags upon bags? We may enlarge our fortunes, but we cannot our bodies; so that it does but spill and run over, whatsoever we take more than we can hold. Our forefathers (by the force of whose virtues we are now supported in our vices) lived every jot as well as we, when they provided and dressed their own meat with their own hands, lodged upon the ground, and were not as yet come to the vanity of gold and gems, when they swore by their earthen gods, and kept their oath, though they died for it. Did not our consuls live more happily when they cooked their own meat with those victorious hands that had conquered so many enemies, and won so many laurels? Did they not live more hap-pily, I say, than our *Apicius* (that corrupter of youth, and plague of the age he lived in) who after he had spent a prodigious fortune upon his belly, poisoned himself for fear of starving, when he had yet 250,000 crowns in his coffers? Which may serve to show us that it is the mind, and not the sum, that makes any man rich, when *Apicius* with all his treasure counted himself in a state of beggary and took poison to avoid that condition, which another would have prayed for. But why do we call it poison, which was the wholesomest draught of his life? His daily gluttony was poison rather, both to himself and others. His ostentation of it was intolerable, and so was the infinite pains he took to mislead others by his example, who went fast enough of themselves without driving.

I T is a shame for a man to place his felicity in those entertainments and appetites that are stronger in brutes. Do not beasts eat with a better stomach? Have they not more satisfaction in their lusts? And they have not only a quicker relish of their pleasures, but they enjoy them without either scandal or remorse. If sensuality were happiness, beasts would be happier than men; but human felicity is lodged in the soul, not in the flesh. They that deliver themselves up to luxury are still either tormented with too little, or oppressed with too much; and equally miserable, by being either deserted or overwhelmed. They are like men in a dangerous sea; one while cast adry upon a rock, and another while swallowed up in a whirlpool; and all this from the mistake of not distinguishing good from evil. The huntsman that with much labour

If sensuality were happiness, beasts would be happier than men

36

and hazard takes a wild beast, runs as great a risk afterward in the keeping of him; for many times he tears out the throat of his master; and it is the same thing with inordinate pleasures. The more in number, and the greater they are, the more general and absolute a slave is the servant of them. Let the common people pronounce him as happy as they please, he pays his liberty for his delights, and sells himself for what he buys.

LET any man take a view of our kitchens, the number of our cooks, and the variety of *We have as* our meats. Will he not wonder to see so *many diseases* much provision made for one belly? We *as dishes* have as many diseases as we have cooks or meats; and the service of the appetite is the study now in vogue. To say nothing of our trains of lackeys, and our troops of caterers, and sewers. Good God! That ever one belly should employ so many people! How nauseous and fulsome are the surfeits that follow these excesses? Simple meats are out of fashion, and all are collected into one; so that the cook does the office of the stomach; nay, and of the teeth too, for the meat looks as if it were chewed beforehand. Here is the luxury of all tastes in one dish, and more like a vomit than a soup. From these compounded dishes arise compounded diseases, which require compounded medicines. It is the same thing with our minds that it is with our tables; simple vices are curable by simple counsels, but a general dissolution of manners is hardly overcome. We are overrun with a public, as well as with a private madness. The physicians of old understood little more than the virtue of some herbs to stop blood, or heal a wound. And their firm and healthful bodies needed little more before they were corrupted by luxury and pleasure. And when it came to that once, their business was not to lay hunger, but to provoke it by a thousand inventions and sauces. That which was aliment to a craving stomach is become a burden to a full one. From hence came paleness, trembling, and worse effects from crudities than famine; a weakness in the joints, the belly stretched, suffusion of choler, the torpor of the nerves, and a palpitation of the heart. To say nothing of migraines, torments of the eyes, and ears; headache, gout, scurvy, several sorts of fevers, and putrid ulcers; with other diseases that are but the punishment of luxury. So long as our bodies were hardened with labour, or tired with exercise or hunting, our food was plain and simple. Many dishes have made many diseases.

IT is an ill thing for a man not to know the measure *Drunkenness* of his stomach, nor to consider that men *is a voluntary* do many things in their drink that they are *madness* ashamed of sober, drunkenness being nothing else but a voluntary madness. It emboldens men to do all sorts of mischiefs; it both irritates wickedness and discovers it; it does not make men vicious, but it shows them to be so. It was in a drunken fit that *Alexander* killed *Clytus*. It makes him that is insolent, prouder; him that is cruel, fiercer; it takes away all shame. He that is peevish breaks out presently into ill words and blows. The lecher, without any regard to decency, or scandal, turns up his whore in the marketplace. A man's tongue trips, his head runs round, he staggers in his pace. To say nothing of the crudities and diseases that follow upon this distemper. Consider the public mischiefs it has done. How many warlike nations, and strong cities, that have stood invincible to attacks and sieges, has drunkenness overcome? Is it not a great honour to drink the company dead? A magnificent virtue to swallow more wine than the rest, and yet at last to be outdone by a hogshead? What shall we say of those men that invert the offices of day and night? As if our eyes were only given us to make use of in the dark. Is it day? *It is time to go to bed.* Is it night? *It is time to rise.* Is it towards morning? *Let us go to supper.* When other people lie down, they rise; and lie till the next night to digest the debauch of the day before. It is an argument of clownery, to do as other people do. Luxury steals upon us by degrees; first, it shows itself in a more than ordinary care of our bodies; it slips next into the furniture of our houses; and it gets then into the fabric, curiosity, and expense of the house itself. It appears, lastly, in the fantastical excesses of our tables. We change and shuffle our meats, confound our sauces, serve that in first that used to be the last, and value our dishes, not for the taste, but for the rarity. Nay, we are so delicate that we must be told when we are to eat or drink; when we are hungry, or weary; and we cherish some vices as proofs and arguments of our happiness. The most miserable mortals are they that deliver themselves up to their palates, or to their lusts. The pleasure is short, and turns presently nauseous, and the end of it is either shame or repentance. It is a brutal entertainment, and unworthy of a man, to place his felicity in the service of his senses. As to the wrathful, the contentious, the ambitious, though the distemper be great, the offence has yet something in it that is manly. But the basest of prostitutes are those that dedicate themselves wholly to lust, what with their hopes and fears, anxiety of thought, and perpetual disquiets, they are never well, full nor fasting.

WHAT a deal of business is now made about our *The folly and* houses and diet, which was at first both *vanity of lux-* obvious and of little expense? Luxury led *ury* the way, and we have employed our wits in the aid of our vices. First we desired superfluities; our next step was to wickedness; and in conclusion, we delivered up our minds to our bodies, and so became slaves to our appetites, which before were our servants, and are now become our masters. What was it that brought us to the extravagance of embroideries, perfumes, tire-women, &c. We passed the bounds of Nature, and lashed out into superfluities; insomuch, that it is nowadays only for beggars and clowns to content themselves with what is sufficient. Our luxury makes us insolent and mad. We take upon us like princes, and fly out for every trifle, as if there were life and death in the case. What a madness is it for a man to lay out an estate upon a table or a cabinet, a patrimony upon a pair of pendants, and to inflame the price of curiosities according to the hazard either of breaking or losing of them? To wear garments that will neither defend a woman's body, nor her modesty; so thin that

40

one would not in all conscience swear that she were not naked: for she hardly shows more in the privacies of her amour than in public. How long shall we covet and oppress, enlarge our possessions, and account that too little for one man which was formerly enough for a nation? And our luxury is as insatiable as our avarice. Where is that lake, that sea, that forest, that spot of land, that is not ransacked to gratify our palate? The very earth is burdened with our buildings; not a river, not a mountain, escapes us. Oh, that there should be such boundless desires in our little bodies! Would not fewer lodgings serve us? We lie but in one, and where we are not, that is not properly ours. What with our hooks, snares, nets, dogs, &c. we are at war with all living creatures; and nothing comes amiss, but that which is either too cheap, or too common; and all this is to gratify a fantastical palate. Our avarice, our ambition, our lusts, are insatiable; we enlarge our possessions; swell our families; we rifle sea and land for matter of ornament and luxury. A bull contents himself with one meadow, and one forest is enough for a thousand elephants; but the little body of a man devours more than all other living creatures. We do not eat to satisfy hunger, but ambition; we are dead while we are alive, and our houses are so much our tombs, that a man might write our *epitaphs* upon our very doors.

A voluptuous person, in fine, can neither be a good man, a good patriot, nor a good friend; for he is transported with his appetites, without considering that the lot of man is the *A voluptuous person cannot be a good man*

41

law of Nature. A good man (like a good soldier) will stand his ground, receive wounds, glory in his scars, and in death itself, love his master for whom he falls; with that divine precept always in his mind, *Follow God*. Whereas he that complains, laments and groans, must yield nevertheless, and do his duty, though in spite of his heart. Now, what a madness is it for a man to choose rather to be lugged than to follow, and vainly to contend with the calamities of human life? Whatsoever is laid upon us by necessity, we should receive generously. For it is foolish to strive with what we cannot avoid. We are born subjects, and to obey God is perfect liberty. He that does this shall be free, safe, and quiet. All his actions shall succeed to his wish: and what can any man desire more than to want nothing from without, and to have all things desirable within himself? Pleasures do but weaken our minds, and send us for our support to fortune, who gives us money only as the wages of slavery. We must stop our eyes and our ears. *Ulysses* had but one rock to fear, but human life has many. Every city, nay, every man is one, and there is no trusting even to our nearest friends. Deliver me from the superstition of taking those things which are light, and vain, for felicities.

CHAPTER 12

AVARICE AND AMBITION ARE
INSATIABLE AND RESTLESS

THE man that would be truly rich must not increase his fortune, but retrench his appetites: for riches are not only superfluous, but mean, and little more to the possessor than to the looker-on. What is the end of ambition and avarice, when at best, we are but stewards of what we falsely call our own? All those things that we pursue with so much hazard and expense of blood, as well to keep as to get, for which we break faith and friendship – what are they but the mere *deposita* of fortune? And not ours, but already inclining toward a new master. There is nothing our own, but that which we give to ourselves, and of which we have a certain, and an impregnable, possession. Avarice is so insatiable that it is not in the power of liberality to content it. And our desires are so boundless that whatever we get is but in the way to getting more without end. And so long as we are solicitous for the increase of wealth, we lose the true use of it, and spend our time in putting out, calling in, and passing our accounts, without any substantial benefit, either to the world or to ourselves. What is the difference betwixt old men and children? The one cries for nuts and apples, and the other for gold and silver. The one sets up courts of justice, hears and determines, acquits and condemns in jest, the other in earnest; the one makes houses of clay, the other of marble: so that the works of old men are nothing in the world but the progress and improvement of children's errors; and they are to be admonished and punished too like children, not in revenge for injuries received, but as a correction of injuries done, and to make them give over. There is some substance yet in gold and silver; but as to judgements and statutes, procuration and continuance-money, these are only the visions and dreams of avarice. Throw a crust of bread to a dog, he takes it open-mouthed, swallows it whole, and presently gapes for more: just so do we with the gifts of fortune; down they go without chewing, and we are immediately ready for another chop. But what has avarice now to do with gold and silver that is so much outdone by curiosities of a far greater value? Let us no longer complain that there was not a heavier load laid upon those precious metals, or that they were not buried deep enough, when we have found out ways by wax and parchments, and by bloody usurious contracts, to undo one another. It is remarkable that Providence has given us all things for our advantage near at hand: but iron, gold and silver (being both the instruments of blood and slaughter, and the price of it), Nature has hidden in the bowels of the earth.

THERE is no avarice without some punishment, over and above that which it is to itself. *Avarice punishes itself* How miserable is it in the desire! How miserable even in the attaining of our ends! For money is a greater torment in the possession than it is in the pursuit. The fear of losing it is a great trouble, the loss of it a greater, and it is made a greater yet by opinion. Nay, even in the case of no direct loss at all, the covetous man loses what he does not get. It is true, the people call the rich man a happy man, and wish themselves in his condition; but can any condition be worse than that which carries vexation and envy along with it? Neither is any man to boast of his fortune, his herds of cattle, his number of slaves, his lands and palaces; for comparing that which he has to that which he further covets, he is a beggar. No man can possess all things, but any man may contemn them, and the contempt of riches is the nearest way to the gaining of them.

SOME magistrates are made for money, and those commonly are bribed with money. We are all turned merchants, and look not in- *Money does all* to the quality of things, but into the price of them; for reward we are pious, and for reward again we are impious. We are honest so long as we may thrive upon it, but if the devil himself give better wages, we change our party. Our parents have trained us up into an admiration of gold and silver, and the love of it is grown up with us to that degree, that when we would show our gratitude to heaven, we make presents of those metals. This is it that makes poverty look like a curse and a reproach, and the poets help it forward – the chariot of the sun must be all of gold, the best of times must be the Golden Age – and thus they turn the greatest misery of mankind into the greatest blessings.

NEITHER does avarice make us only unhappy in ourselves, but malevolent also to mankind. The soldier

Avarice makes us ill-natured as well as miserable wishes for war, the husbandman would have his corn dear, the lawyer prays for dissension, the physician for a sickly year, he that deals in curiosities, for luxury and excess — each makes up his fortunes out of the corruptions of the age. High winds and public conflagrations make work for the carpenter and bricklayer, and one man lives by the loss of another; some few, perhaps, have the fortune to be detected, but they are all wicked alike. A great plague makes work for the sexton, and, in one word, whosoever gains by the dead has not much kindness for the living. *Demades* of *Athens* condemned a fellow that sold necessaries for funerals, upon proof that he wished to make himself a fortune by his trade, which could not be but by a great mortality. But perhaps he did not so much desire to have many customers, as to sell dear and buy cheap; besides, all of that trade might have been condemned as well as he. Whatsoever whets our appetites, flatters and depresses the mind, and by dilating it, weakens it; first blowing it up, and then filling and deluding it with vanity.

TO proceed now from the most prostitute of all *The cares and crimes that attend ambition* vices, sensuality and avarice, to that which passes in the world for the most generous, the thirst of glory and dominion. If they that run mad after wealth and honour could but look into the hearts of them that have already gained these points, how would it startle them to see those hideous cares and crimes that wait upon ambitious greatness; all those acquisitions that dazzle

46

the eyes of the vulgar are but false pleasures, slippery and uncertain. They are achieved with labour, and the very guard of them is painful. Ambition puffs us up with vanity and wind; and we are equally troubled, either to see anybody before us, or nobody behind us, so that we lie under a double envy; for whosoever envies another is also envied himself. What matters it how far *Alexander* extended his conquests, if he was not yet satisfied with what he had? Every man wants as much as he covets; and it is lost labour to pour into a vessel that will never be full. He that had subdued so many princes and nations, upon the killing of *Clytus* (one friend) and the loss of *Hephestion* (another), delivered himself up to anger and sadness; and when he was master of the world, he was yet a slave to his passions. Look into *Cyrus, Cambyses*, and the whole *Persian* line, and you shall not find so much as one man of them that died satisfied with what he had gotten. Ambition aspires from great things to greater, and propounds matters even impossible, when it has once arrived at things beyond expectation. It is a kind of dropsy; the more a man drinks, the more he covets. Let any man but observe the tumults and the crowds that attend palaces; what affronts must we endure to be admitted, and how much greater when we are in? The passage to virtue is fair, but the way to greatness is craggy, and it stands not only upon a precipice, but upon ice too; and yet it is a hard matter to convince a great man that his station is slippery, or to prevail with him not to depend upon his greatness, but all superfluities are hurtful. A rank crop lays the corn; too great a burden

47

of fruit breaks the bough; and our minds may be as well overcharged with an immoderate happiness. Nay, though we ourselves would be at rest, our fortune will not suffer it: the way that leads to honour and riches leads to trouble; and we find the causes of our sorrows in the very objects of our delights. What joy is there in feasting and luxury, in ambition and a crowd of clients, in the arms of a mistress, or in the vanity of an unprofitable knowledge? These short and false pleasures deceive us; and, like drunkenness, revenge the jolly madness of *one* hour with the nauseous and sad repentance of *many*. Ambition is like a gulf, everything is swallowed up in it and buried, beside the dangerous consequence of it. For that which one has taken from all, may be easily taken away again by all from one. It was not either virtue or reason, but the mad love of a deceitful greatness that animated *Pompey* in his wars, either abroad or at home. What was it but his ambition that hurried him to *Spain*, *Africa*, and elsewhere, when he was too great already in everybody's opinion but his own? And the same motive had *Julius Cæsar*, who could not, even then, brook a superior himself, when the commonwealth had submitted unto two already. Nor was it any instinct of virtue that pushed on *Marius*, who, at the head of an army was himself yet led on under the command of ambition: but he came at last to the deserved fate of other wicked men, and to drink himself of the same cup that he had filled to others. We impose upon our reason when we suffer ourselves to be transported with titles, for we know that they are nothing but a more glorious sound; and so for ornaments and gildings, though there may be a lustre to dazzle our eyes, our understanding tells us yet that it is only outside, and that the matter under it is only coarse and common.

I will never envy those that the people call great and happy. A sound mind is not to be shaken with a popular and vain applause, *Miserable are those people* nor is it in the power of their pride to dis- *that the world* turb the state of our happiness. An honest *accounts great and happy* man is known nowadays by the dust he raises upon the way, and it is become a point of honour to overrun people and keep all at a distance, though he that is put out of the way may perchance be happier than he that takes it. He that would exercise a power profitable to himself, and grievous to nobody else, let him practise it upon his passions. They that have burnt cities, otherwise invincible, driven armies before them and bathed themselves in human blood; after that they have overcome all open enemies, they have been vanquished by their lust, by their cruelty, and without any resistance. *Alexander* was possessed with the madness of laying kingdoms waste. He began with *Greece*, where he was brought up, and there he quarried himself upon that in it which was best; he enslaved *Lacedemon* and silenced *Athens*: nor was he content with the destruction of those towns which his father *Philip* had either conquered or bought, but he made himself the enemy of human nature, and like the worst of beasts, he worried what he could not eat. Felicity is an unquiet thing; it torments itself, and puzzles the brain. It makes some people ambitious, others

49

luxurious; it puffs up some, and softens others; only (as it is with wine) some heads bear it better than others. But it dissolves all. Greatness stands upon a precipice; and if prosperity carries a man ever so little beyond his poise, it overbears and dashes him to pieces. It is a rare thing for a man in a great fortune to lay down his happiness gently; it being a common fate for a man to sink under the weight of those felicities that raise him. How many of the nobility did *Marius* bring down to herdsmen, and other mean offices? Nay, in the very moment of our despising servants, we may be made so ourselves.

CHAPTER 13

HOPE AND FEAR ARE THE BANE OF
HUMAN LIFE

NO man can be said to be perfectly happy that runs the risk of disappointment, which is the case of every man that *fears* or *hopes* for anything. For *hope* and *fear*, how distant soever they may seem to be the one from the other, they are both of them yet coupled in the same chain, as the guard and the prisoner; and the one treads upon the heels of the other. The reason of this is obvious, for they are passions that look forward, and are ever solicitous for the future; only *hope* is the more plausible weakness of the two, which in truth, upon the main, are inseparable, for the one cannot be without the other: but where the *hope* is stronger than the *fear*, or the *fear* than the *hope*, we call it the one or the other. For without *fear*, it were no longer *hope*, but *certainty*; as without *hope*, it were no longer *fear*, but *despair*. We may come to understand, whether our disputes are vain or no, if we do but consider that we are either troubled about the *present*, the *future*, or *both*. If the present, it is easy to judge, and the future is uncertain. It is a foolish thing to be miserable beforehand for fear of misery to come; for a man loses the present which he might enjoy, in expectation of the future. Nay, the fear of losing anything is as bad as the loss itself. I will be as prudent as I can, but not timorous or careless: and I will bethink myself, and forecast what inconveniences may happen before they come. It is true, a man may fear, and yet not be fearful; which is no more than to have the affection of fear without the vice of it; but yet a frequent admittance of it runs into a habit. It is a shameful and unmanly thing to be doubtful, timorous, and uncertain – to set one step forward and another backward – and to be irresolute. Can there be any man so fearful that had not rather fall once than hang always in suspense?

OUR miseries are endless, if we stand in fear of all possibilities; the best way in such a case is to drive out one nail with another, and a little to qualify fear with hope, which may serve to palliate a misfortune, though not to cure it. There is not anything that we fear, which is so certain to come, as it is certain that many things which we do fear will not come; but we are loath to oppose our credulity when it begins to move us, and so to bring our fear to the test. Well! But, *What if the thing we fear should come to pass?* Perhaps it will be the better for us. Suppose it to be *death* itself, why may it not prove the glory of my life? Did not poison make *Socrates* famous? And was not *Cato's* sword a great part of his honour? *Do we fear any misfortune to befall us?* We are not presently sure that it will happen. How many deliverances have come unlooked for? And how many mischiefs that we looked for, have never come to pass? It is time enough to lament when it comes, and, in the *interim*, to promise ourselves the best. What do I know but something or other may delay or divert it? Some have escaped out of the fire; others, when a house has

Our miseries are endless if we fear all possibilities

fallen over their head, have received no hurt: one man
has been saved when a sword was at his throat; another has been condemned, and outlived his heads-
man: so that ill fortune, we see, as well as good, has
her levities: peradventure it will be, peradventure not;
and until it comes to pass, we are not sure of it. We do
many times take words in a worse sense than they
were intended, and imagine things to be worse taken
than they are. It is time enough to bear a misfortune
when it comes, without anticipating it.

HE that would deliver himself from all apprehensions of the future, let him first take for
granted that all his fears will fall upon him, *Prepare for*
the worst
and then examine and measure the evil that
he fears, which he will find to be neither great nor
long. Beside, that the ills which he fears he may suffer,
he suffers in the very fear of them. As in the symptoms
of an approaching disease, a man shall find himself lazy
and listless; a weariness in his limbs, with a yawning
and shuddering all over him. So it is in the case of a
weak mind; it fancies misfortunes, and makes a man
wretched before his time. Why should I torment myself at present with what perhaps may fall out fifty
years hence? This humour is a kind of voluntary disease, and an industrious contrivance of our own un-
happiness, to complain of an affliction that we do not
feel. Some are not only moved with grief itself, but
with the mere opinion of it; as children will start at a
shadow, or at the sight of a deformed person. If we
stand in fear of violence from a powerful enemy, it is
some comfort to us that whosoever makes himself

terrible to others is not without fear himself. The least
noise makes a lion start, and the fiercest of beasts,
whatsoever enrages them, makes them tremble too: a
shadow, a voice, an unusual odour, rouses them.

THE things most to be feared, I take to be of three
kinds: *want*, *sickness*, and those *violences*

*The things most
to be feared are
want, sickness,
and the violences
of men in power*

that may be imposed upon us by a *strong
hand*. The last of these has the greatest
force, because it comes attended with
noise and tumult; whereas the incom-
modities of poverty and diseases are more natural, and
steal upon us in silence, without any external circumstances of horror. But the other marches in pomp,
with fire and sword, gibbets, racks, hooks; wild beasts
to devour us; stakes to impale us; engines to tear us to
pieces; pitched bags to burn us in, and a thousand
other exquisite inventions of cruelty. No wonder
then, if that be the most dreadful to us, that presents
itself in so many uncouth shapes; and by the very so-
lemnity is rendered the most formidable. The more
instruments of bodily pain the executioner shows us,
the more frightful he makes himself. For many a man
that would have encountered death in any generous
form, with resolution enough, is yet overcome with
the *manner* of it. As for the calamities of hunger and
thirst, inward ulcers, scorching fevers, tormenting fits
of the stone, I look upon these miseries to be at least as
grievous as any of the rest; only they do not so much
affect the fancy, because they lie out of sight. Some
people talk high of dangers at a distance; but (like
cowards) when the executioner comes to do his duty,

and show us the fire, the axe, the scaffold, and death at hand, their courage fails them upon the very pinch, when they have most need of it. Sickness (I hope), captivity, fire, are no new things to us; the falls of houses, funerals, and conflagrations are every day before our eyes. The man that I supped with last night is dead before morning. Why should I wonder then, seeing so many fall about me, to be hit at last myself? What can be a greater madness than to cry out, *Who would have dreamed of this?* And why not, I beseech you? Where is that estate that may not be reduced to beggary? That dignity which may not be followed with banishment, disgrace, and extreme contempt? That kingdom that may not suddenly fall to ruin; change its master, and be depopulated? That prince that may not pass the hand of a common hangman? That which is one man's fortune may be another's; but the foresight of calamities to come breaks the violence of them.

CHAPTER 14

IT IS ACCORDING TO THE TRUE OR FALSE ESTIMATE OF THINGS THAT WE ARE HAPPY OR MISERABLE

HOW many things are there that the fancy makes terrible by night, which the day turns into ridiculous? What is there in labour, or in death, that a man should be afraid of? They are much slighter in act than in contemplation; and we *may* contemn them, but we *will* not: so that it is not because they are hard that we dread them, but they are hard because we are first afraid of them. Pains, and other violences of fortune, are the same thing to us that goblins are to children: we are more scared with them than hurt. We take up our opinions upon trust, and err for company, still judging that to be best that has most competitors. We make a false calculation of matters, because we advise with opinion, and not with Nature; and this misleads us to a higher esteem for riches, honour, and power, than they are worth: we have been used to admire and recommend them, and a private error is quickly turned into a public. The greatest and the smallest things are equally hard to be comprehended; we account many things *great*, for want of understanding what effectually is so: and we reckon other things to be *small*, which we find frequently to be of the highest value. Vain things only move vain minds. The accidents that we so much bog-

gle at are not terrible in themselves, but   ade
so by our infirmities, but we consult rat.   ve
hear than what we feel, without examining   ,
or discussing the things we fear; so that
stand still and tremble, or else directly run
those troops did, that upon the raising of the
took a flock of sheep for the enemy. When the
and mind are corrupted, it is no wonder if all things
prove intolerable; and not because they are so in truth,
but because we are dissolute and foolish: for we are
infatuated to such a degree, that betwixt the common
madness of men, and that which falls under the care of
the physician, there is but this difference: the one labours of a disease, and the other of a false opinion.

THE *Stoics* hold that all those torments that commonly draw from us groans and ejacula- *Let every man*
tions, are in themselves trivial and con- *make the best*
temptible. But these high-flown expres- *of his lot*
sions apart (how true soever), let us discourse the point
at the rate of ordinary men, and not make ourselves
miserable before our time; for the things we appre-
hend to be at hand may possibly never come to pass.
Some things trouble us more than they should, other
things sooner; and some things again disorder us that
ought not to trouble us at all; so that we either
enlarge, or create, or anticipate our disquiets. For the
first part, let it rest as a matter in controversy, for that
which I account light, another perhaps will judge insupportable. One man laughs under the lash, and another whines for a fillip. How sad a calamity is poverty
to one man, which to another appears rather desirable

than inconvenient? For the poor man, who has nothing to lose, has nothing to fear: and he that would enjoy himself to the satisfaction of his soul, must be either poor indeed, or at least look as if he were so. Some people are extremely dejected with sickness and pain, whereas *Epicurus* blessed his fate with his last breath, in the acutest torments of the stone imaginable. And so for banishment, which to one man is so grievous, and yet to another is no more than a bare change of place, a thing that we do every day for our health, pleasure, nay, and upon the account even of common business. How terrible is death to one man, which to another appears the greatest providence in Nature, even toward all ages and conditions? It is the wish of some, the relief of many, and the end of all. It sets the slave at liberty, carries the banished man home, and places all mortals upon the same level: insomuch that life itself were punishment without it. When I see tyrants, tortures, violences, the prospect of death is a consolation to me, and the only remedy against the injuries of life.

NAY, so great are our mistakes in the true estimate of things that we have hardly done *Our very* anything that we have not had reason to *prayers many* wish undone, and we have found the *times are curses* things we feared to be more desirable than those we coveted. Our very prayers have been more pernicious than the curses of our enemies, and we must pray again to have our former prayers forgiven. Where is the wise man that wishes to himself the wishes of his mother, nurse, or his tutor; the worst of enemies, with the intention of the best of friends? We are undone if their prayers be heard, and it is our duty to pray that they may not; for they are no other than well-meaning execrations. They take evil for good, and one wish fights with another. Give me rather the contempt of all those things whereof they wish me the greatest plenty. We are equally hurt by some that pray for us, and by others that curse us: the one imprints in us a false fear, and the other does us mischief by a mistake. So that it is no wonder if mankind be miserable when we are brought up from the very cradle under the imprecations of our parents. We pray for trifles without so much as thinking of the greatest blessings, and we are not ashamed many times to ask God for that which we should blush to own to our neighbour.

IT is with us as with an innocent that my *father* had in his family; she fell blind on a sudden, *We are vain* and nobody could persuade her she was *and wicked,* blind. *She could not endure the house* (she *and will not* cried) *it was so dark,* and was still calling to *believe it* go abroad. That which we laughed at in her, we find to be true in ourselves, we are covetous and ambitious; but the world shall never bring us to acknowledge it, and we impute it to the place: nay, we are the worse of the two; for that blind fool called for a guide, and we wander about without one. It is a hard matter to cure those that will not believe they are sick. We are ashamed to admit a master, and we are too old to learn. Vice still goes before virtue: so that we have two works to do; we must cast off the one, and learn the other. By one evil we make way to another, and

59

only seek things to be avoided, or those of which we are soon weary. That which seemed too much when we wished for it, proves too little when we have it, and it is not as some imagine, that felicity is greedy, but it is little, and narrow, and cannot satisfy us. That which we take to be very high at a distance we find to be but low when we come at it. And the business is, we do not understand the true state of things: we are deceived by rumours; when we have gained the thing we aimed at, we find it to be either ill or empty; or perchance less than we expect, or otherwise perhaps great, but not good.

CHAPTER 15

THE BLESSINGS OF TEMPERANCE
AND MODERATION

THERE is not anything that is necessary to us, but we have it either *cheap* or *gratis*; and this is the provision that our Heavenly Father has made for us, whose bounty was never wanting to our needs. It is true, the belly craves and calls upon us, but then a small matter contents it: a little bread and water is sufficient, and all the rest is but superfluous. He that lives according to reason shall never be poor, and he that governs his life by opinion shall never be rich: for Nature is limited, but fancy is boundless. As for meat, clothes, and lodging, a little feeds the body and as little covers it: so that if mankind would only attend human nature, without gaping at superfluities, a cook would be found as needless as a soldier: for we may have necessaries upon very easy terms; whereas we put ourselves to great pains for excesses. When we are cold, we may cover ourselves with skins of beasts; and against violent heats we have natural grottoes; or with a few osiers and a little clay we may defend ourselves against all seasons. Providence has been kinder to us than to leave us to live by our wits, and to stand in need of invention and arts. It is only pride and curiosity that involve us in difficulties: if nothing will serve a man but rich clothes and furniture, statues and plate, a numerous train of servants, and the rarities of all nations, it is not fortune's fault, but his own, that he is not satisfied: for his desires are insatiable, and this is not a thirst, but a disease; and if he were master of the whole world, he would be still a beggar. It is the mind that makes us rich and happy, in what condition soever we are; and money signifies no more to it than it does to the gods. If the religion be sincere, no matter for the ornaments: it is only luxury and avarice that make poverty grievous to us; for it is a very small matter that does our business; and when we have provided against cold, hunger and thirst, all the rest is but vanity and excess: and there is no need of expense upon foreign delicacies, or the artifices of the kitchen. What is he the worse for poverty, that despises these things? Nay, is he not rather the better for it, because he is not able to go to the price of them? For he is kept sound whether he will or no: and that which a man *cannot* do, looks many times as if he *would not*.

WHEN I look back into the moderation of past *The modera-* ages, it makes me ashamed to discourse, as *tion of past* if poverty had need of any consolation. *ages* For we are now come to that degree of intemperance that a fair patrimony is too little for a meal. *Homer* had but one servant, *Plato* three, and *Zeno* (the master of the masculine sect of *Stoics*) had none at all. The daughters of *Scipio* had their portions out of the common treasury, for their father left them not worth a penny: how happy were their husbands that had the people of *Rome* for their father-in-law! Shall any man now contemn poverty after these eminent examples, which are sufficient not only to justify, but to recommend it? Upon *Diogenes'* only servant running away from him, he was told where he was and persuaded to fetch him back again. *What*, says he, *can* Manes *live without* Diogenes, *and not* Diogenes *without* Manes? And so let him go. The piety and moderation of *Scipio* has made his memory more venerable than his arms; and more yet after he left his country than while he defended it: for matters were come to that pass, that either *Scipio* must be injurious to *Rome*, or *Rome* to *Scipio*. Coarse bread and water to a temperate man is as good as a feast; and the very herbs of the field yield a nourishment to man as well as to beasts. It was not by choice meats and perfumes that our forefathers recommended themselves, but by virtuous actions, and the sweat of honest, military, and of manly labours.

WHILE Nature lay in common, and all her benefits were promiscuously enjoyed, what could be happier than the state of mankind, when people lived without avarice or envy? *The state of innocence* What could be richer than when there was not a poor man to be found in the world? So soon as this impartial bounty of Providence came to be restrained by covetousness, and that particulars appropriated that to themselves which was intended for all, then did poverty creep into the world, when some men by desiring more than came to their share, lost their title to the rest. A loss never to be repaired; for though we may come yet to get much, we once had all. The fruits of the earth were in those days divided among the inhabitants of it, without either want or excess. So long as men contented themselves with their lot, there was no violence, no engrossing or hiding of those benefits for particular advantages which were appointed for the community; but every man had as much care for his neighbour as for himself. No arms or bloodshed, no war, but with wild beasts: but under the protection of a wood or a cave, they spent their days without cares, and their nights without groans; their innocence was their security and their protection. There were as yet no beds of state, no ornaments of pearl or embroidery, nor any of those remorses that attend them; but the heavens were their canopy, and the glories of them their spectacle. The motions of the orbs, the courses of the stars, and the wonderful order of Providence, was their contemplation. There was no fear of the house falling, or the rustling of a rat behind the *arras*; they had no palaces then like cities: but they had open air, and breathing-room, crystal fountains, refreshing shades, the meadows dressed up in their native beauty, and such cottages as were according to Nature, and wherein they lived contentedly, without fear either of losing or of falling. These people lived without either solitude or fraud, and yet I must call them rather happy than wise. That men were generally better before they were corrupted than after, I make no doubt; and I am apt to believe that they were both stronger and hardier too, but their wits were not yet come to maturity; for Nature does not give virtue, and it is a kind of art to become good. They had not as yet torn up the bowels of the earth for gold, silver, or precious stones; and so far were they from killing any man, as we do, for a spectacle, that they were not as yet come to it, either in fear or anger; nay, they spared the very fishes. But after all this, they were innocent because they were ignorant; and there is a great difference betwixt not knowing how to offend and not being willing to do it. They had, in that rude life, certain images and resemblances of virtue, but yet they fell short of virtue itself, which comes only by institution, learning, and study, as it is perfected by practice. It is indeed the end for which we were born, but yet it did not come into the world with us; and in the best of men, before they are instructed, we find rather the matter and the seeds of virtue, than the virtue itself. It is the wonderful benignity of Nature that has laid open to us all things that may do us good, and only hid those things from us that may hurt us: as if she durst not trust us with gold and silver, or with iron, which is the instrument of war and contention for the other. It is we ourselves that have drawn out of the earth both the *causes* and the *instruments* of our dangers: and we are so vain as to set the highest esteem upon those things to which Nature has assigned the lowest place. What can be more coarse and rude in the mine than these precious metals, or more slavish and dirty than the people that dig and work them? And yet they defile our minds more than our bodies, and make the possessor fouler than the artificer of them. Rich men, in fine, are only the greater slaves. Both the one and the other wants a great deal.

HAPPY is that man that eats only for hunger, and drinks only for thirst; that stands upon his own legs, and lives by *A temperate life is a happy life*

65

reason, not by example; and provides for use and necessity, not for ostentation and pomp. Let us curb our appetites, encourage virtue, and rather be beholden to ourselves for riches than to fortune, who when a man draws himself into a narrow compass, has the least mark at him. Let my bed be plain and clean, and my clothes so too; my meat without much expense, or many waiters, and neither a burden to my purse, nor to my body; nor to go out the same way it came in. That which is too little for luxury is abundantly enough for Nature. The end of eating and drinking is satiety. Now, what matters it though one eats and drinks more, and another less, so long as the one is not a-hungry, nor the other a-thirst? *Epicurus*, that limits pleasure to Nature, as the *Stoics* do virtue, is undoubtedly in the right; and those that cite him to authorise their voluptuousness do exceedingly mistake him, and only seek a good authority for an evil cause: for their pleasures of sloth, gluttony and lust, have no affinity at all with his precepts or meaning. It is true, that at first sight his philosophy seems effeminate; but he that looks nearer him will find him to be a very brave man only in a womanish dress.

IT is a common objection, I know, that these philosophers do not live at the rate they talk; for they can flatter their superiors, gather estates, and be as much concerned at the loss of fortune or of friends, as other people: as sensible of reproaches, as luxurious in their eating and drinking, their furniture, their houses; as magnificent in their plate, servants and officers; as profuse and cu-

Let philosophers live as they teach

rious in their gardens, &c. Well! And what of all this, or if it were twenty times more? It is some degree of virtue for a man to condemn himself; and if he cannot come up to the best, to be yet better than the worst; and if he cannot wholly subdue his appetites, however to check and diminish them. If I do not live as I preach, take notice that I do not speak of myself, but of virtue; nor am I so much offended with other men's vices as with my own. All this was objected to *Plato*, *Epicurus*, *Zeno*: nor is any virtue so sacred as to escape malevolence. The *Cynic Demetrius* was a great instance of severity and mortification; and one that imposed upon himself neither to possess anything, nor so much as to ask it: and yet he had this *scorn* put upon him, that his profession was *poverty*, not *virtue*. *Plato* is blamed for *asking* money, *Aristotle* for *receiving* it, *Democritus* for *neglecting* it, *Epicurus* for *consuming* it. How happy were we if we could but come to imitate these men's vices; for if we knew our own condition, we should find work enough at home. But we are like people that are making merry at a play or a tavern when their own houses are on fire, and yet they know nothing of it. Nay, *Cato* himself was said to be a drunkard; but *drunkenness* itself shall sooner be proved to be no crime, than *Cato* dishonest. They that demolish temples and overturn altars show their good will, though they can do the gods no hurt; and so it fares with those that invade the reputation of great men. If the professors of virtue be as the world calls them, avaricious, libidinous, ambitious, what are they then that have a detestation for the very name of it? But malicious natures do not want wit to abuse men more honest than themselves. It is the practice of the multitude to bark at eminent men, as little dogs do at stranges; for they look upon other men's virtues as the upbraiding of their own wickedness. We should do well to commend those that are good; if not, let us pass them over; but however let us spare ourselves; for besides the blaspheming of virtue, our rage is to no purpose. But to return now to my text.

WE are ready enough to limit others, but loath to *It is good to pra-* put bounds and restraint upon ourselves; *ctise frugality in* though we know that many times a *plenty* greater evil is cured by a less; and the mind that will not be brought to virtue by precepts, comes to it frequently by necessity. Let us try a little to eat upon a joint-stool, to serve ourselves, to live within compass, and accommodate our clothes to the end they were made for. Occasional experiments of our moderation give us the best proof of our firmness and virtue. A well-governed appetite is a great part of liberty; and it is a blessed lot, that since no man can have all things that he would have, we may all of us forbear desiring what we have not. It is the office of Temperance to overrule us in our pleasures: some she rejects, others she qualifies and keeps within bounds. Oh, the delights of rest, when a man comes to be weary; and of meat, when he is heartily hungry! I have learned (says our author) by one journey, how many things we have that are superfluous, and how easily they may be spared; for when we are without them, upon necessity, we do not so much as feel the want of them. This is the second blessed day (says he) that my friend and I have travelled together; one wagon carries ourselves and our servants; my mattress lies upon the ground, and I upon that; our diet answerable to our lodging; and never without our figs and our table-books. The muleteer without shoes, and the mules only prove themselves to be alive by their walking. In this equipage, I am not willing, I perceive, to own myself, but as often as we happen into better company, I presently fall a-blushing, which shows that I am not yet confirmed in those things which I approve and commend. I am not yet come to own my frugality, for he that is ashamed to be seen in a mean condition would be proud of a splendid one. I value myself upon what passengers think of me, and tacitly renounce my principles; whereas I should rather lift up my voice to be heard by mankind, and tell them, *You are all mad; your minds are set upon superfluities, and you value no man for his virtues.* I came one night weary home, and threw myself upon the bed, with this consideration about me: *There is nothing ill that is well taken.* My baker tells me he has no bread; but, says he, you may get some of your tenants, though I fear it is not good. No matter, said I, for I will stay until it be better; that is to say, until my stomach will be glad of worse. It is discretion sometimes to practise temperance, and wont ourselves to a little; for there are many difficulties both of time and place, that may force us upon it. When we come to the matter of patrimony, how strictly do we examine what every man is worth before we will trust him with a penny: *Such a man*, we

69

cry, *has a great estate, but it is shrewdly encumbered; a very fair house, but it was built with borrowed money; a numerous family; but he does not keep touch with his creditors; if his debts were paid, he would not be worth a groat.* Why do we not take the same course in other things, and examine what every man is worth? It is not enough to have a long train of attendants, vast possessions, or an incredible treasure in money and jewels; a man may be poor for all this. There is only this difference at best; one man borrows of the *usurer*, and the other of *fortune*. What signifies the carving or gilding of the chariot; is the master ever the better for it?

WE cannot close up this chapter with a more gen-

The modera- erous instance of moderation than that of
tion and brave- *Fabricius. Pyrrhus* tempted him with a sum
ry of Fabricius of money to betray his country; and
Pyrrhus' physician offered *Fabricius*, for a sum of money, to poison his *master*. But he was too brave, either to be overcome by gold, or to overcome by poison; so that he refused the money, and advised *Pyrrhus* to have a care of treachery; and this in the heat too of a licentious war. *Fabricius* valued himself upon his poverty, and was as much above the thought of riches as of *poison. Live,* Pyrrhus, says he, *by my friendship; and turn that to thy satisfaction, which was before thy trouble,* that is to say, that *Fabricius* could not be corrupted.

CHAPTER 16

CONSTANCY OF MIND GIVES A MAN REPUTATION, AND MAKES HIM HAPPY IN DESPITE OF ALL MISFORTUNE

THE whole duty of man may be reduced to the two points of *abstinence* and *patience*; *temperance* in *prosperity*, and *courage* in *adversity*. We have already treated of the former, and the other follows now in course.

EPICURUS will have it, that a wise man will *bear* all *injuries*; but the *Stoics* will not allow those things to be *injuries* which *Epicurus* calls so. Now, betwixt *these two*, there is the *A wise man is above injuries* same difference that we find betwixt two *gladiators*; the one receives wounds, but yet maintains his ground; the other tells the people, when he is in blood, that *It is but a scratch*, and will not suffer anybody to part them. An *injury* cannot be *received*, unless it be *done*: but it may be *done*, and yet not *received*; as a man may be in the water and not swim, but if he swims, it is presumed that he is in the water. Or if a blow or a shot be levelled at us, it may so happen that a man may miss his aim, or some accident interpose that may divert the mischief. That which is hurt is passive, and inferior to that which hurts it; but you will say, that *Socrates* was condemned and put to death, and so received an injury; but I answer, that the tyrants *did* him an injury, and yet he *received* none. He that steals anything from me and hides it in my own house, though I have not lost it, yet he has stolen it. He that lies with his own wife, and takes her for another woman, though the woman be honest, the man is an adulterer. Suppose a man gives me a draught of poison and it proves not strong enough to kill me; his guilt is never the less for the disappointment. He that makes a pass at me is as much a murderer, though I put it by, as if he had struck me to the heart. It is the intention, not the effect, that makes the wickedness. He is a thief that has the will of killing and slaying, before his hand is dipped in blood; as it is sacrilege, the very intention of laying violent hands upon holy things. If a philosopher be exposed to torments, the axe over his head, his body wounded, his guts in his hands, I will allow him to groan; for virtue itself cannot divest him of the nature of a man; but if his mind stands firm, he has discharged his part. A great mind enables a man to maintain his station with honour; so that he only makes use of what he meets in his way, as a pilgrim that would fain be at his journey's end.

IT is the excellency of a great mind to *ask* nothing, and to *want* nothing; and to say, *I will have nothing to do with fortune, that repulses Cato, and prefers* Vatinius. He that quits his hold, and accounts anything good that is not honest, runs gaping after casualties, spends his days in anxiety and vain expectation: that man is miserable. And yet it is hard, you will say, to be banished or cast into prison; nay, what if it were to be burnt, or any other way destroyed? We have examples

A great man neither asks anything, nor wants anything

72

in all ages, and in all cases, of great men that have tri-
umphed over all misfortunes. *Metellus* suffered *exile*
resolutely, *Rutilius* cheerfully. *Socrates* disputed in the
dungeon; and though he might have made his escape,
refused it, to show the world how easy a thing it was
to subdue the two great terrors of mankind, *death* and
a *jail*. Or what shall we say of *Mucius Scævola*, a man
only of a military courage, and without the help either
of philosophy or letters, who, when he found that he
had killed the secretary instead of *Porfenna* (the prince),
burnt his right hand to ashes for the mistake, and held
his arm in the flame until it was taken away by his very
enemies? *Porfenna* did more easily pardon *Mucius* for
his intent to kill him than *Mucius* forgave *himself* for
missing of his aim. He might have a luckier thing, but
never a braver.

DID not *Cato*, in the last night of his life, take *Plato*
to bed with him, with his sword at his
bedhead; the one that he might have death
at his will, the other, that he might have it
Cato's
constancy
in his power; being resolved that no man should be
able to say either that he killed or that he saved *Cato*?
So soon as he had composed his thoughts, be took his
sword; *Fortune*, says he, *I have hitherto fought for my
country's liberty and for my own, and only that I might live
free among freemen; but the cause is now lost, and* Cato *safe.*
With that word he cast himself upon his sword; and
after the physicians, that pressed in upon him, had
bound up his wound, he tore it open again, and so
expired with the same greatness of soul that he lived.
But these are the examples, you will say, of men

73

famous in their generations. Let us but consult history, and we shall find, even in the most effeminate of nations, and the most dissolute of times, men of all degrees, ages, and fortunes, nay, even women themselves, that have overcome the fear of death: which, in truth, is so little to be feared, that duly considered, it is one of the greatest benefits in Nature. It was as great an honour for *Cato*, when his party was broken, that he himself stood his ground, as it would have been if he had carried the day, and settled a universal peace: for it is an equal prudence to make the best of a bad game, and to manage a good one. The day that he was *repulsed*, he *played*; and the night that he *killed* himself, he *read*, as valuing the loss of his life, and the missing of an office at the same rate. People, I know, are apt to pronounce upon other men's infirmities by the measure of their own, and to think it impossible that a man should be content to be burnt, wounded, killed, or shackled, though in some cases he may. It is only for a great mind to judge of great things; for otherwise, that which is our infirmity will seem to be another body's; as a straight stick in the water appears to be crooked. He that yields, draws upon his own head his own ruin, for we are sure to get the better of fortune if we do but struggle with her. Fencers and wrestlers we see what blows and bruises they endure, not only for honour, but for exercise. If we turn our backs once, we are routed and pursued. That man only is happy that draws good out of evil, that stands fast in his judgement, and unmoved with any external violence: or however, so little moved, that the keenest arrow in the quiver of fortune is but as the prick of a needle to him rather than a wound: and all her other weapons fall upon him only as hail upon the roof of a house that crackles and skips off again, without any damage to the inhabitant.

A generous and clear-sighted young man will take it for a happiness to encounter ill fortune. It is nothing for a man to hold up his head in a calm; but to maintain his post when all others have quitted their ground, and *The greatest evil in adversity is the submitting to it* there to stand upright, where other men are beaten down, this is divine and praiseworthy. What ill is there in torments, or in those things which we commonly account grievous crosses? The great evil is the want of courage, the bowing and submitting to them, which can never happen to a wise man; for he stands upright under any weight: nothing that is to be borne displeases him; he knows his strength, and whatsoever may be any man's lot, he never complains of, if it be his own. Nature, he says, deceives nobody; she does not tell us whether our children shall be fair or foul, wise or foolish, good subjects or traitors, nor whether our fortune shall be good or bad. We must not judge of a man by his ornaments, but strip him of all the advantages and the impostures of fortune; nay, of his very body too, and look into his mind. If he can see a naked sword at his eyes without so much as winking; if he make it a thing indifferent to him whether his life go out at his throat or at his mouth; if he can hear himself sentenced to torments or exiles, and under the very hand of the executioner, says thus to himself, *All*

75

this I am provided for, and it is no more than a man that is to suffer the fate of humanity. This is the temper of mind that speaks a man happy; and without this, all the confluences of external comforts signify no more than the personating of a king upon the stage; when the curtain is drawn, we are players again. Not that I pretend to exempt a wise man out of the number of men, as if he had no sense of pain. But I reckon him as compounded of body and soul: the body is irrational, and may be galled, burnt, tortured; but the rational part is fearless, invincible, and not to be shaken. This is it that I reckon upon as the supreme good of man; which, until it be perfected, is but an unsteady agitation of thought; and in the perfection, an immovable stability. It is not in our contentions with fortune, as in those of the theatre, where we may throw down our arms and pray for quarter: but here we must die firm and resolute. There needs no encouragement to those things which we are inclined to by a natural instinct, as the preservation of ourselves with ease and pleasure; but, if it comes to the trial of our faith by torments, or of our courage by wounds, these are difficulties that we must be armed against by philosophy and precept. And yet all this is no more than what we were born to, and no matter of wonder at all; so that a wise man prepares himself for it, as expecting whatsoever *may be, will be.* My body is frail and liable not only to the impressions of violence, but to afflictions also, that naturally succeed our pleasures. Full meals bring crudities; whoring and drinking make the hands to shake and the knees to tremble. It is only the surprise and newness of the thing which makes that misfortune terrible, which by premeditation might be made easy to us. For that which some people make light by sufferance, others do by foresight. Whatsoever is necessary, we must bear patiently. It is no new thing to die; no new thing to mourn; and no new thing to be merry again. Must I be *poor*? I shall have company. In *banishment*? I will think myself born there. If I *die*, I shall be no more sick; and it is a thing I can do but once.

LET us never wonder at anything we are born to; for no man has reason to complain, where we are all in the same condition. He that escapes might have suffered; and it is but equal to submit to the law of mortality. We *Let no man be surprised with what he is born to* must undergo the colds of winter, the heats of summer, the distempers of the air, and the diseases of the body. A wild beast meets us in one place, and a man that is more brutal in another; we are here assaulted by fire, there by water. *Demetrius* was reserved by Providence for the age he lived in, to show that neither the times could corrupt him, nor he reform the people. He was a man of an exact judgement, steady to his purpose, and of a strong eloquence; not finical in his words, but his sense was masculine and vehement. He was so qualified in his life and discourse, that he served both for an example, and a reproach. If fortune should have offered that man the government, and the possession of the whole world, upon condition not to lay it down again, I dare say he would have refused it: and thus have expostulated the matter with you: *Why should you tempt a freeman to put his shoulder under a bur-*

den; or an honest man to pollute himself with the dregs of mankind? Why do you offer me the spoils of princes and of nations, and the price not only of your blood, but of your souls? It is the part of a great mind to be temperate in prosperity, resolute in adversity; to despise what the vulgar admire, and to prefer a mediocrity to an excess. Was not *Socrates* oppressed with poverty, labour, nay and the worst of wars in his own family, a fierce and turbulent woman to his wife? Were not his children indocile, and like their mother? After seven and twenty years spent in arms, he fell under the slavery to the *Thirty Tyrants*, and most of them his bitter enemies. He came at last to be sentenced as *a violater of religion, a corrupter of youth, and a common enemy to God and man.* After this, he was imprisoned and put to death by poison, which was all so far from working upon his mind that it never so much as altered his countenance. We are to bear ill accidents as unkind seasons, distempers, or diseases; and why may we not reckon the actions of wicked men even among those accidents? Their deliberations are not counsels, but frauds, snares, and inordinate motions of the mind; and they are never without a thousand pretences, and occasions of doing a man mischief. They have their informers, their knights of the post; they can make an interest with powerful men, and one may be robbed as well upon the bench as upon the highway. They lie in wait for advantages, and live in perpetual agitation betwixt hope and fear; whereas he that is truly composed will stand all shocks, either of violences, flatteries, or menaces, without perturbation. It is an inward fear that makes us curious after what we hear abroad.

IT is an error to attribute either *good* or *ill* to *fortune*, but the *matter* of it we may; and we ourselves are the occasion of it, being in effect the artificers of our own happiness or misery; for the mind is above fortune; *The works of fortune are neither good nor evil* if that be evil, it makes everything else so too: but if it be right and sincere, it corrects what is wrong, and mollifies what is hard, with modesty and courage. There is a great difference among those that the world calls wise men. Some take up private resolutions of opposing fortune, but they cannot go through with them; for they are either dazzled with splendour on the one hand, or affrighted with terrors on the other: but there are others that will close and grapple with fortune, and still come off victorious. *Mucius* overcame the fire; *Regulus*, the gibbet; *Socrates*, poison; *Rutilius*, banishment; *Cato*, death; *Fabricius*, riches; *Tubero*, poverty; and *Sextius*, honours. But there are some again so delicate, that they cannot so much as bear a scandalous report; which is the same thing as if a man should quarrel for being jostled in a crowd, or dashed as he walks in the streets. He that has a great way to go must expect a slip, to stumble, and to be tired. To the luxurious man, frugality is a punishment; labour and industry, to the sluggard; nay, study itself is a torment to him: not that these things are hard to us by Nature, but we ourselves are vain and irresolute: nay, we wonder, many of us, how any man can live without wine, or endure to rise so early in a morning.

79

A brave man must expect to be tossed; for he is to

Virtue is steer his course in the teeth of fortune, and
glorious in to work against wind and weather. In the
extremities suffering of torments, though there appears
but one virtue, a man exercises many. That which is
most eminent is patience (which is but a branch of fortitude). But there is prudence also in the choice of the
action, and in the bearing what we cannot avoid; and
there is constancy in bearing it resolutely: and there is
the same concurrence also of several virtues in other
generous undertakings. When *Leonidas* was to carry his
300 men into the Straits of *Thermopylæ*, to put a stop to
Xerxes' huge army: *Come, fellow soldiers*, says he, *eat
your dinners here, as if you were to sup in another world.*
And they answered his resolution. How plain and im-
perious was that short speech of *Cæditius* to his men
upon a desperate action! And how glorious a mixture
was there in it both of bravery and prudence! *Soldiers*,
says he, *it is necessary for us to go, but it is not necessary for
us to return.* This brief and pertinent harangue was
worth ten thousand of the frivolous cavils and distinc-
tions of the schools which rather break the mind than
fortify it; and when it is once perplexed, and pricked
with difficulties and scruples, there they leave it. Our
passions are numerous and strong, and not to be mas-
tered with quirks and tricks, as if a man should under-
take to defend the cause of God and Men with a bul-
rush. It was a remarkable piece of honour and policy
together, that action of *Cæsar's*, upon the taking of
Pompey's cabinet at the battle of *Pharsalia*: it is probable
that the letters in it might have discovered who were

80

his friends, and who his enemies; and yet he burnt it
without so much as opening it: esteeming it the no-
blest way of pardoning, to keep himself ignorant both
of the offender and of the offence. It was a brave pres-
ence of mind also in *Alexander*, who, upon advice that
his physician *Philip* intended to poison him, took the
letter of advice in one hand, and the cup in the other,
delivering *Philip* the letter to read, while he himself
drank the potion.

SOME are of the opinion that death gives a man
courage to support pain, and that pain
fortifies a man against death. But I say
rather that a wise man depends upon himself against both, and that he does not either suffer
with patience in hopes of death, or die willingly because he is weary of life; but he bears the one, and
waits for the other, and carries a divine mind through
all the accidents of human life. He looks upon faith
and honesty as the most sacred good of mankind, and
neither to be forced by necessity, nor corrupted by
reward: kill, burn, tear him in pieces, he will be true to
his trust: and the more any man labours to make him
discover a secret, the deeper will he hide it. Resolution
is the inexpugnable defence of human weakness, and it
is a wonderful Providence that attends it. *Horatius Co-
cles* opposed his single body to the whole army, until
the bridge was cut down behind him, and then leaped
into the river with his sword in his hand, and came off
safe to his party. There was a fellow questioned about
a plot upon the life of a tyrant, and put to the torture
to declare his confederates: he named them, one by

Virtue is invincible

one, all the tyrants friends that were about him; and still as they were named, they were put to death: the tyrant asked him at last if there were any more. Yes, says he, you yourself were in the plot; and now you have never another friend left you in the world: whereupon the tyrant cut the throats of his own guards. *He is the happy man that is the master of himself, and triumphs over the fear of death, which has overcome the conquerors of the world.*

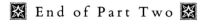 End of Part Two

Seneca on Providence,
Moderation, and Constancy of Mind
Roger L'Estrange and Keith Seddon
Published by Keith Seddon at Lulu 2010
© 2010 Keith Seddon
ISBN 978-0-955-6844-9-4 (paperback)

Typeset in Bembo Book by the editor using Microsoft Word 2007.
Proofs checked and reviewed in Portable Document Format
created using open source PDFCreator 1.0.2.

NOTE ON THE TYPEFACE

All text is set in Bembo Book, designed by Robin Nicholas.

'Originally drawn by Monotype in 1929, the Bembo® design was inspired by the types cut by Francesco Griffo and used by Aldus Manutius in 1495 to print Cardinal Bembo's tract *De Aetna*. A beautiful design with tall ascending lowercase and elegant letterforms, Bembo has been a favourite for book setting for over 70 years. ... Considered by many to be one of Stanley Morison's finest achievements during his tenure as Typographical Advisor to the Monotype Corporation, Bembo has consistently been a bestselling typeface, both in its original hot metal form and in today's digital formats. ... This new digital version of Bembo, called Bembo Book, has been designed to be more suited to text setting in the size range from 10 point to 18 point. Based on the hot metal 10/18 point drawings, which were used to cut all sizes from 10 point to 24 point, this new face has been carefully drawn to produce similar results to those achieved from the hot metal version when letterpress printed. The project started in 2002 when a high quality UK printing house asked for a digital version of Bembo which would give a similar appearance on the page to the 13 point hot metal they were currently using. Hot metal drawings were digitised and extensive editing was carried out on the resultant outlines to ensure that design features and overall colour from the digital output remained close to that of the letterpress product. The resultant typeface is slightly narrower than existing digital versions of Bembo, it is a little more economical in use and gives excellent colour to continuous pages of text. Ascending lowercase letters are noticeably taller than capitals, giving an elegant, refined look to the text.'

(Slightly abridged from http://www.monotype.co.uk/bembo/)

Lightning Source UK Ltd.
Milton Keynes UK
UKOW02f1025190317
296961UK00001B/54/P